RESPECT IN THE WORKPLACE

YOU HAVE TO GIVE IT TO GET IT

ERIC HARVEY

TRISH TAYLOR

D1503041

RESPECT IN THE WORKPLACE
You Have to Give it to Get it

The Walk The Talk Company
P.O. Box 210996
Bedford, TX 76095
Or email us at info@walkthetalk.com

ISBN: 978-1-885228-97-0

Credits

Copy Editor

Kathleen Green, Positively Proofed, Plano TX

info@PositivelyProofed.com

Cover Design

Melissa Farr, Back Porch Creative, Frisco TX
info@BackPorchCreative.com

ISBN 978-1-885228-97
900

9 781885 228970

Respect

re·spect /ri-'spekt/

respect from the Latin *respectus*—to look back at, regard or consider

Noun

A feeling of high regard, thoughtfulness, civility, admiration, esteem, consideration

Example:

I have the greatest respect for my manager.

Verb

To admire a person or object, to value, cherish, honor, to hold in high regard

Example:

I respect her capacity to see all sides of an important issue.

CONTENTS

INTRODUCTION

If you have picked up this book, you have already demonstrated that you care about respect in the workplace. Maybe you are concerned that it is lacking, or that it has disappeared, and you are keen to find ways to get it back.

In the following chapters, you will find actionable, practical and simple methods that can work in any organization. You will learn how to encourage and develop respect with simple, tried and tested tips that can help bring respect back to your workplace. If you are already engaging in good practices, you will learn how they can be enhanced and developed.

What Exactly Is Workplace Respect?

A workplace where everyone is respected and valued is likely to be one where people enjoy being at work. A good workplace where the word on the street is that they treat their staff well is one that employees will be proud to tell everyone about, as well as go the extra mile.

Respect comes from our attitudes and behaviors. It is about how we treat each other and how we make people feel. This can come from the way we speak to people, the way we listen or don't, our body language and the way we talk about others when they are not there. Respect is about good manners—doing the right thing, the things we hopefully learned in school and from our parents. Respect is recognizing that we are all living, breathing, feeling humans who should be treated with dignity.

Think about how you are around those you like or want to impress, or how you might behave on a first date or a job interview. You are (hopefully) polite, looking your best, prepared and paying attention.

Respect means different things to different people and varies within communities and cultures. What was considered acceptable behavior or language a decade ago may be different today.

And doing something because "that's the way we have always done it" will not cut it in today's workplace. Respect means being open to new ways of thinking and accepting that just because a word or behavior doesn't bother us personally doesn't mean that it might be disrespectful to another. Dignity is part of what gives us our humanity. To have respect for others, we must treat them with dignity.

66 Moral authority comes from following universal and timeless principles like honesty, integrity, treating people with respect."

— STEPHEN COVEY

Most of the ways to practice respect are not difficult. It doesn't have to cost you or your organization anything, doesn't take much if any time and doesn't require special training, techniques, gadgets or resources. You can help make your workplace a more civil, human and caring organization with less stress—somewhere people want to spend their time.

So, let's learn how respect is good for business.

You will discover how to exercise more respectful behavior and attitudes with your:

Co-workers

New team members

Manager

Direct reports

Customers

And in meetings, and in other workplace and life situations

When it comes to RESPECT, you need to remember the law of reciprocity...

You Have to Give it to Get it!

WORKPLACE RESPECT IS CRITICAL — HOW TO MAKE SURE IT HAPPENS

> Every human being, of whatever origin, of whatever station, deserves respect. We must each respect others even as we respect ourselves."
>
> — RALPH WALDO EMERSON

It is often said we must earn respect. Though true, you have to give it to get it. Rather than waiting around for someone to earn our respect, we will learn in this book to give respect to everyone, right out of the gate. Yes, you heard correctly, everyone in your workplace gets respect whether you sometimes believe it's deserved or not. The idea that respect must be earned can lead to people being disrespectful to those they believe have not yet earned it. At what point do we think we are ready to deserve respect? Who decides who is worthy? Planning to respect everyone in the workplace, without exception, is the first step in creating a place where everyone will want to respect others.

A Respectful Workplace Will Encourage and Demonstrate:

- A positive attitude
- Communication
- Kindness
- Courtesy
- Listening
- Safety and security
- Good working conditions
- Inclusivity
- Team spirit—a sense of belonging
- Dignity

Remember: Demonstrating workplace respect is not only the right thing to do, but it is also...

Good for Business

To have a team that works well together, it is necessary for members to respect each other. It is also vitally important that management show respect to those who work for them. A survey of over 20,000 people published in the Harvard Review found that respect was the most important thing that a leader could demonstrate.

> " Being treated with respect was more important to employees than recognition and appreciation, communicating an inspiring vision, providing useful feedback—even opportunities for learning, growth and development."
>
> — CHRISTINE PORATH

Productivity rises when there is more respect in the workplace and people are happier. Doesn't that sound like it's worth a little effort on everyone's part?

We spend about a third of our time at work. That's often more than we get to spend with our family, our children and our friends. What happens when we are at our place of employment and the way we feel about our work has a massive impact on our well-being and the work we do. A happy workplace is somewhere that employees want to be, where they have no reason to call out, leave early, or not perform to their best potential. And a happy workplace is one where each person feels respected and respects others.

Defining the Organization's Culture and Values

When an organization has a defined set of values and operating principles, it is easier for everyone to know what is expected of them. Many new progressive businesses have innovative hiring practices because they are determined to hire the brightest and the best. They deliberately have a lengthy hiring and onboarding process to make sure they get the right fit. Some also give workers an opportunity to quit without penalty to maintain their organization's values. Although not every organization can run their business this way, a clearly stated understanding of the mission and values can help avoid the costly mistake of rehiring.

Choose Your Attitude Every Day

Respect comes from having a good attitude. We have to "choose" our attitude and bring that good attitude into the workplace, not once in a while but on a consistent basis. Circumstances can change minute by minute, yet our attitude should not change with it. Learning to adjust our attitude so we can stay in "respect mode" is something that may have to be learned. Having someone with a bad attitude fly off the handle at work, stomp around or lose their temper is uncomfortable for everyone around.

Choosing our attitude means making a conscious decision to feel good, to want to be at work and enjoy the experience. "Fake it 'til you make it" really works. When we change our body to act "as if," our physiology mirrors it. Standing up straight looks more confident than slouching, and you will find that you feel better. Did you know that faking a smile makes the owner of that smile feel happier? The physical shift sets off a chain reaction and an expectation within our body that something good is happening. If you go into work expecting a bad day, that is exactly what you will get. Making a choice to be positive is a powerful first step to gaining self-respect.

Staying Up-to-Date with Trainings and Accreditation

Feeling good about the work we do and being confident that we are doing it well can have a powerful impact on self-respect. Plan to attend available training, online classes or seminars, and then share what you learned with your co-workers.

Respecting Others Through Compliments

As you learn the power of self-respect, you can spread this in the workplace. Complimenting others is great for increasing respect. Compliments do not have to be about personal appearance—a genuine compliment about someone's work will probably be better received and more appropriate. Compliments can also be a way of recognizing that someone has more experience than you.

Ideas for Work-based Compliments

"I am really impressed with how well you handled that difficult customer. I wouldn't have known what to say."

"I appreciate how tech-savvy you are. Can you show me how to recover a document I lost?"

"I see that task is taking time. Don't worry. It's complicated and you are catching on faster than many do."

Training in Respect?

It may seem unnecessary to need training about how to respect others, yet for some it may not come as easily as it should. Instead of training being forced on people in response to a problem, it is far more effective if training in respect is pre-emptive and sets the standard in an organization.

In the following chapters, you will find ideas for

everyone in your organization to learn easy and often fun ways to get the respect you and your co-workers deserve. Although some ideas are specific to situations, these ideas are for any area of life.

Action Items

- Choose your attitude
- Give respect to everyone you meet
- Align yourself with your company's values

RESPECT FOR CO-WORKERS

We have established that we spend a lot of time with our co-workers. We often get to know them as friends outside of work. Yet a workplace brings together a whole gamut of personalities. We meet people who may never cross our paths in life outside of work. We interact with those from different backgrounds, age groups, genders, religions, abilities, interests and political beliefs. Although you may be lucky enough to develop lifelong friendships at work, there may also be people you have no desire to know beyond the workplace. Nothing says you have to become friends with your co-workers, yet a happy and thriving workplace requires a level of respect among the team. Respect includes all the ways that we interact with each other, the way we work, how we share information and the way in which we speak to and about each other. We all have a responsibility to play our part in helping develop cohesion within the team.

I'm Just Too Busy!

For the overwhelmed and underappreciated, being encouraged to be more respectful in the workplace might seem like just one more thing to put on your plate. Actually, it's the opposite. When you see that more respect equals more productivity, you will be less stressed and more able to do your job better. Imagine if you feel comfortable in asking for help when you are close to a deadline or when you aren't stressing over all the little annoyances that can distract you from your work.

If busyness is the problem, then lack of respect or failing to make sure it exists is likely to make you busier. A workplace where employees feel disrespected is unlikely to hold onto good people. Hiring new team members is costly and time consuming. When everyone works together and is invested in creating and maintaining a respectful workplace for everyone, you can relax a little, feeling secure in your role. A team where everyone supports and encourages each other brings a sense of calm and can make work a pleasure.

Respect sets an expectation that the workplace is a positive place to be and that everyone will play their part and also share in the rewards of a job well done. When a project is complete and each person on the team feels valued and included, they are more likely to be more productive the next time. Being left out, discouraged or disrespected has the opposite effect. When team members are invested in the work at hand, knowing they are integral to its success, they are more likely to step up, no matter what.

If you listen to the speeches at a movie awards show, the laundry list of people thanked might seem boring if you are only interested in seeing the movie stars. Yet, without the team of scriptwriters, editors, producers and costume and set designers, the star would not be standing where they are. The success is a team effort, and this list of names is the recognition and respect shown to those who are a vital part of the team who helped create that success. None of us are an island—we need each other.

So how can we stay happy and respectful at work when we are all so different? Stay away from "hot button" issues. Intelligent debate is one thing, yet because these have the potential to develop into angry tirades, it is much safer not getting started. It is unlikely that you will change anyone's mind about their position. While you are trying to prove your point, you are getting hot under the collar and no work is getting done. These issues are best avoided in the workplace.

66 Consider how hard it is to change yourself and you'll understand what little chance you have in trying to change others."

— JACOB M. BRAUDE

Avoid Cliques

Being respectful means including people. The workplace can be a stimulating and enjoyable place, or it can be reminiscent of high school. Look out for the co-worker who doesn't get included. Help them feel like they're part of the team.

10 Ways to Respect Your Co-workers

1. Be generous with your time and the things you know.

Being prepared to give up information for the good of the team helps everyone. Yes, information is power, yet respect means letting go of power-play games and working for the good of the team.

2. Keep a clean desk and work area.

Make sure to clean up after yourself in public areas.

3. Avoid gossip.

This is a good way to be respectful and protect yourself. Yet you can also go one step further. If you are in a situation and you hear gossip or witness workplace bullying, the brave and respectful thing to do is to speak up. Being silent when you observe poor workplace behavior or harassment makes you complicit and part of the problem instead of the solution. You do not have to get into arguments or debates. A simple "I prefer not to be part of this conversation when X is not here to defend themselves" or "I have always found X to be most pleasant and I find it better not to engage in gossip" will remove you from the negative situation.

4. Keep everyone informed and up to date.

A common complaint in workplaces is "but nobody told me." Being out of the loop can be annoying and also bad for business. If a deadline changes or a meeting is rescheduled, failing to inform a team member can be bad for the bottom line. Making sure that lines of communication are clear and up to date will help avoid potential problems down the line.

5. Be fair.

If it is necessary for someone to work holidays or weekends, be prepared to take your turn. The same applies to taking preferred lunch breaks. Make sure that everyone gets a fair chance.

6. Respect the universal "I'm working" signal.

This is especially true in shared or open-plan offices. If a co-worker is wearing headphones, that often means they are focused on their work. In today's workplace, a team member might be engaged in an international call, viewing a webinar or taking an online test.

7. Respect your co-workers' time.

Don't forward or copy them on unnecessary emails or send jokes to everyone in the office. Respect that others may have a different workload. Use discretion before disturbing your co-workers. Learn to recognize the unwritten and written cues. If you are not sure, ask. It can take up to 20 minutes to get back into the flow of work after a disruption or distraction. Check your co-workers' preferred method of receiving communication. Do they prefer email, phone calls, texts or for you to speak to them in person at a convenient time?

8. Give credit to anyone you work with for their part in your success.

Taking credit for another person's work or claiming their ideas as your own is not the sign of a good team player. Giving credit is an easy way to encourage the sharing of information and an openness within the work environment. The opposite of this is secrecy. If team members feel the need to keep their work secret from each other to avoid the stealing of ideas, it encourages mistrust and suspicion. Shared information and ideas allow creativity to flow. It may surprise you how many more ideas you can come up with if you are willing to share them. And, when it comes to respect, always remember that you have to give it to get it!

9. Mind your language.

What is appropriate at home, among your friends or at a social event may not be suitable for the workplace. Cursing and bad language can be offensive to those within earshot. Be aware of what comes out of your mouth. Cultural differences can mean that words that are acceptable in some places may be received differently in others. YouTube and Instagram stars may curse with impunity, yet in most workplaces you will soon discover that it will draw attention to you for the wrong reasons.

10. Common areas—leave only footprints.

We often have to share areas in the workplace, which is a great opportunity to practice giving respect to get it. Be mindful of how your behavior affects others. Practice "situational awareness": Leave areas as you find them. Even more preferable: Leave them better than you find them.

Five Low-Cost, High-Impact Ways You Can Demonstrate Respect to Team Members

1. Bring breakfast—cookies, donuts, bagels or a fruit bowl. People love unexpected treats.
2. Check in on people, find out how their day is going, ask if there is anything you can do to help.
3. Compliment someone or ask genuine questions about their life outside of work. Interesting people are interested people.
4. Share useful information. Have a source who can get you a bargain, special deals or movie or sports tickets? Share the love and tell the team.
5. Pay attention to your team and be on the lookout for signs that people are struggling. People may have concerns and have no one to tell. Make time for them.

A Special Team Member

Geoff was the handyman and the gardener for a small community college. He wasn't a part of the decision-making team. He wasn't the boss and he didn't attend meetings. Yet he made a difference to every person who attended the workplace. Why? Because he was the first to arrive at work in the morning. On days when it snowed, he cleared the driveway so that team members could park safely. He was always waiting with a hot cup of coffee for those who had been stuck in traffic or had a stressful journey. They respected him and he respected everyone else. He didn't say, "It's not my job." He said, "How can I help?"

66 One of the most sincere forms of respect is actually listening to what another has to say."

— BRYANT H. MCGILL

Action Items

- Look for opportunities to be generous and kind
- Leave only footprints
- Stop and think about how your behavior affects others

RESPECT FOR NEW TEAM MEMBERS

Can you remember what it felt like to be the new kid on the block? Entering a new workplace can be a daunting experience. No matter how confident you are when starting a new position, it is almost always stressful. If it has been awhile since you were the new kid, you may have forgotten what it feels like. After being successful and relaxed in a previous position, you are thrown into the deep end. Everyone knows more than you do. You don't know the written rules, much less the unwritten ones. Everyone is curious about you, and it's hard to know how to behave. A confident adult can suddenly be psychologically and emotionally pulled back into feeling like a child on the first day of elementary school.

Take yourself back in time for a moment. Think of a time when you were brand-new and felt awkward in your new position, standing around and feeling like a spare part. What should you do next? Who do you ask? Starting a new job is a vulnerable position to be in. At one of the times in life when all you want to do is fit in and impress your new boss and team, you are often nervous, stressed and possibly even scared. Now think of a time when you started a new job and it went well. What was the difference? What were the processes that made sure you feel comfortable and confident from the beginning?

Let's think of some ideas to help ease your new hire into their position. Whether you are the boss or the co-worker, you can be part of the process. People learn and perform better when they are relaxed and feel welcome. A task that is obvious to you because you have been doing it for a long time might be daunting to a new hire. Making their first days easy is a good thing to do. It creates a better chance that you will get a confident teammate who can be supportive and help make your job better. Some ways to welcome a new member are obvious: Being kind, courteous and friendly are the easy ones. What else can you do to make sure the new kid is still with you at the end of their first week and has not run for the hills?

Don't Judge

A new hire might be awkward and uncomfortable and therefore unable to be themselves at first. When we are trying to fit in, we often overcompensate and come across all wrong. Have you ever met someone who you didn't like at first and then, as you got to know them, became friends? Give them a chance. Don't write a new person off before they've had a chance to shine.

Have a Plan

There is often a lot of paperwork involved in becoming a new hire. Even though it is important, most of it is for the organization and not the team member. Even if your organization has an official employee handbook, consider having one sheet of paper with vital information that a new hire should know—a Welcome to the Team memo that lays out the simplest "need to know" items. Plowing through a 100-page handbook in the first week is daunting and the most important items are often missed. What is noteworthy or happening that week or month that you really want them to be aware of?

Your new addition to the team needs to know what to do at each step of the training period, as well as knowing who to ask if they run out of things to do. Give them tasks they can do in-between their core work so they are not left worried about what to do next. Be clear who they report to. If there is more than one person, make sure the priority is laid out. One of the most common complaints from new hires is that they are pulled in many directions and don't know who they should ask or tell.

Create a Welcoming Space

Make sure they have a space they can call their own, even if it is just a place to put their lunch, purse or belongings. Make sure they have somewhere to sit and work.

Ladies and Gentlemen, May I Present....

Consider assigning a buddy who can show them around and make introductions, or have a "Welcome to the Team" luncheon. It doesn't have to be anything formal but just a way you can quickly and painlessly integrate the new hire into the team.

Be Patient and Remember Your Attitude

Whether you are part of the training process, showing the new team member around, or simply meet them in passing, be kind and patient. Being the new hire can be painful. Everyone has been there, yet it is easy to forget what those first weeks and months were like. Allowing the "newbie" to ask as many questions as they need without feeling they are taking up your time will make them feel as though they're a part of the team and help them learn quickly.

Be Positive...About the Team and the Entire Organization

Avoid sharing gossip or stories about other team members. A random comment at the start of a new job can color a person's view. Focus only on the positive qualities of each team member and encourage the new hire to seek out the best person when they have questions. There will always be things to complain about if you look for them. A new person entering the workplace needs to feel encouraged and believe they made the right decision in taking their new job. They don't need to know all of the organization's problems and struggles before finding their footing.

Communicate

Be sure to share any information that might be considered an unwritten rule (and consider if this can become a written one in the future). Many things that are common practice to the seasoned employee can be very confusing to a new hire.

Be Open to Their Ideas

A new perspective is a gift. Allow them to make suggestions. They may see things you have long since stopped noticing. Ask about their last job, their likes and dislikes. Help them feel at home.

Be Kind

One of the difficulties of being new in any situation is that it has the potential to knock your confidence. Starting over knowing nothing is awkward, and no one wants to feel awkward. Be ready to offer support and encouragement if the new person is struggling. Ask how you can help, and let them know that you have their back.

Get to Know Them

This is a real-life person in front of you. Find out who they are, ask questions and find something you have in common. Show them that working with you can be enjoyable. Where do you hang out after work? Who brings in the best cookies? Which of your team members has specific skills and talents that may be helpful to your new team member? Make sure they know that you enjoy your work. Include them in anything that is happening so they can begin to feel a part of the team as soon as possible.

Peanuts

No, not the amount you are being paid. Actual peanuts. There was a time when peanut allergies, like many other allergies, were seen as the domain of sensitive snowflakes. Now it's known that a peanut allergy can be fatal. It is not only respectful but vital that we are aware of the needs and issues that may affect our teammates, as well as how we can make efforts to keep them safe and happy. If your new co-worker has specific needs—whether it's in relation to their food or anything relating to their personal needs—be as respectful as you can to accommodate them. Respect is thinking about the other person and doing our best to make provisions for them. This sometimes means going out of our way.

You may hear people say that respect is treating everyone the same. This is not always true. Making sure that everyone gets an equal chance in the workplace means treating them fairly. A person with a disability or a special need might need to be given special accommodations to ensure they get an equal opportunity in the workplace.

> 66 R-E-S-P-E-C-T. Find out what it means to me."

— ARETHA FRANKLIN

When You Are the New Kid

As the new hire, you also have a responsibility to make sure you do what you can to fit in with your new team.

Don't Be Like Jim

Jim had a habit of sending multiple emails within seconds of each other with questions about every tiny detail. It may have come from his insecurity in his new job. By the end of the first week, his new teammates were exasperated by his constant barrage of questions, many of which he could have figured out by reading the staff handbook or by simply using common sense.

If You Are a New Team Member

Avoid Saying…"we used to do it this way in my old workplace." If you have a great idea that you believe could be an asset, wait until you have settled in before offering your opinions. No one wants to be told what to do by the "new kid on the block." Listen, pay attention, be ready to learn, take notes. You will not be expected to remember everything in the first few days. Take responsibility for your own learning and success.

66 We must learn to live together as brothers or perish together as fools."

— MARTIN LUTHER KING JR.

Bullying or Just a Prank?

In some workplaces, there is a history and culture of prank-playing on those new to their job. Even if you experienced it when you started working, it is not acceptable behavior in today's workplace. Just as dangerous "hazing" practices have been all but outlawed and eradicated from schools and colleges, playing pranks on a new worker is no longer acceptable workplace behavior. Would you treat someone like this if you respected them?

Bullying in the workplace requires a zero-tolerance approach. This is much easier to implement when organizational values are clearly laid out in policies and procedures.

Again, communication among teams from the start is vital. A workplace that encourages respect does more than pay lip service to a policy; they show it at all levels in trainings, behaviors and language, and it includes everyone. If you see a new teammate being bullied, made fun of or being treated anything less than respectfully, then it is your duty to call it out.

66 Respect your fellow human being, treat them fairly, disagree with them honestly, enjoy their friendship, explore your thoughts about one another candidly, work together for a common goal and help one another achieve it."

— BILL BRADLEY

Action Items

- Be welcoming
- Be patient
- Be positive
- Don't judge; give them a chance to shine

DEMONSTRATING RESPECT FOR YOUR MANAGER

66 By working faithfully eight hours a day,
you may eventually get to be the boss
and work 12 hours a day."

— ROBERT FROST

Managers get a bad rap in some workplaces. It's
entirely possible that they may work longer hours
than the people reporting to them and not get
much more pay. Managers are also often moved
into their position without formal training in
management and may do their best despite
limited guidelines. The buck stops with them.
When things go wrong, they get criticism from all
sides. Being the leader can sometimes be a lonely
and thankless place to be. Respecting your

manager may not be something you think about very often. They sit in their corner office, with all the perks. Why do they need respect? Well, just like everyone else in the workplace, they are people doing a job, and they respond to respect (or lack thereof) in exactly the same way. Deciding that you will have a great attitude in your interactions with your manager will go a long way in creating a mutually respectful relationship.

They can't read your mind if there is something bothering you and you don't communicate it. That doesn't mean they don't care. Put yourself in their shoes and realize that they may have solid reasons for decisions and behaviors. They are not just out to annoy you or ruin your day. Your manager may be dealing with a no-win situation. The answer may seem obvious to you, yet they must factor in many other issues that you are unaware of. You can support your manager in doing their job by showing them respect, which will help develop a professional relationship of mutual respect.

12 Ways to Win Over Your Manager

1. Complete your work on time and follow the rules.

This includes paperwork such as timecards and leave requests. There is only one of you. If you realized how all the little tasks add up, you might have a little empathy for your manager. If you make a mistake and it needs straightening out, that might not seem like such a big deal. Imagine chasing after another 10, 15 or even dozens of people to make sure they did their job. These are the things that have managers chasing their tails and working weekends to ensure you get paid.

2. Ask questions to make sure you understand the tasks you are assigned.

Making sure that you don't waste time going down the wrong route will benefit you, the team and your manager. Clarify what is expected and be sure you know when it needs to be completed.

3. Check if there is anything else that needs to be done before leaving for the day.

Are there other roles you could take on to help your team during busy periods? When deadlines loom, if you are not an integral part of the core work, see if there is something that you can do to be supportive.

4. Realize that you may not see the whole picture.

Your manager may not always have the luxury of sharing all of the information during an ongoing project or situation. Sometimes you may need to exercise patience and wait for an answer or decision.

5. Be interested in your manager as a person.

Being in charge can be an isolating existence. Managers don't always get recognition for the work they do.

6. Be supportive. Don't talk behind your boss's back and create divisions.

You don't have to be your boss's best friend, yet you don't have to be their enemy, either. Don't listen to or share negative stories about your manager. Instead, share how they have supported or encouraged you.

7. Keep confidences.

If your manager confides work-related information with you, keep that to yourself (unless you are sure it is for public knowledge).

8. Be a problem solver, not a problem creator.

If you have a problem, come up with solutions and suggestions when possible rather than offering up problems and complaints. Before you knock on their door asking a question or making a complaint, ask yourself, "Have I done my research? Have I done everything possible to figure this out by myself?"

9. Be flexible in your duties.

Be open to tackling tasks outside of your job description. This will make you more valuable to your manager. You may also find another role that will help you in your future. Volunteer to attend trainings and conferences, chair meetings or take on new responsibilities. It can only enhance your work and résumé and widen your experience.

10. Every manager is different.

Your current or new manager may have a different style than your last one. That doesn't make it wrong. Get used to different ways of doing things. Being open to new ways of working makes you more adaptable and a valued team player.

11. What to do when meeting with the boss.

If you are called into the office, take a notepad. Be prepared to listen, ask questions and take notes. Be sure that you are clear about any information or assigned tasks you are given.

12. Get to know their routine and preferences.

Is your boss a morning person? Are they better approached after they have had their coffee? Do they give you signs and signals that make it clear they do not want to be disturbed? Are there critical times of the day, week or month when it would be a bad time to make requests? Do they respond better to verbal or written information?

A small, nonprofit team was working on a funding deadline that was taking longer than expected. The complex financial details could not be done by everyone, yet the team mobilized and made sure that everyone helped. There was no unimportant job that evening. Duties such as printing, making copies and providing drinks and snacks were highly valued. When the project was successfully completed, the whole team that had taken part and stayed late to help was afforded the same respect. It also created a feeling of camaraderie and belonging that everyone was glad to be a part of.

Performance Reviews

At some point, your manager will probably have to give you a performance review. These can be stressful for everyone involved, yet there are things you can do to make it easier on both you and your manager.

- Be prepared and do whatever is necessary in advance so the meeting is as painless as possible.

- Be honest with yourself. If you do this, you will know what to expect and there will not be any surprises. If you are hoping for a good review and you know in your heart that you have not worked or produced as well as you could have, be realistic.
- Don't take it personally. If you have a positive and honest relationship with your manager, the appraisal is a good opportunity for learning and growth.
- Ask what you can do better. Look for positive outcomes and opportunities. If you have areas that need strengthening, ask for further training or opportunities that will stretch you.
- Always learn and grow.

A Few Words from a Manager

"What I Ask of You"

Appreciate the fact that my work is no easier than yours. I've got a tough job, too. Tasks often look:

Easier than they are … especially when somebody else has to do them. Don't assume the worst of

Me. You don't wake up in the morning asking, "How can I make life miserable for someone today?" Well, neither do I. If you have a problem with something I've done (or haven't done), talk to me about it instead of talking to others. Continue to

Perform your job as best you can. That will make it easier for me to do the same.

Adopt the mindset that to be successful at work, you need me as much as I need you.

Assume half

The responsibility for our working relationship. If we work well together, take half the credit. If we don't, accept half the responsibility for making it better. Remember that I'm

Human. Before you judge me or decide how you'll work with me, walk awhile in my shoes. If

You do, I think you'll find …

With more understanding, we can meet in the middle and walk the rest of the way together.

— From *Walk Awhile in My Shoes*, by Eric Harvey and Steve Ventura

Action Items

- Do your work and ask what else you can do
- Put yourself in their shoes
- Be supportive
- Remember that they are human, too

RESPECT TECHNIQUES FOR SUPERVISORS AND MANAGERS

Rewards and Recognition Lead to Retention

When workers are respected and adequately rewarded and recognized, they perform well, and everyone wins. Rewards do not have to be expensive. In fact, a reward that has monetary value yet no thought behind it might have the opposite impact. A business known for giving expensive gifts to workers at Christmas, though generous, did not display respect because the gifts were seemingly chosen randomly and did not take into account the individual team members' interests or preferences. Getting to know an employee, putting your head around the corner occasionally and asking about their life could be more respectful than buying them a showy piece of jewelry not to their taste or the latest bells-and-whistles gadget they may already own.

A mixture of both rewards and recognition can go a long way in creating employee retention.

When a team member is named Employee of the Month or receives other recognition, it can be worth more than a financial reward. Knowing that someone is seeing what you do and valuing your contribution builds self-esteem and fosters a sense of belonging in the workplace.

In the TV show *Undercover Boss*, company owners secretly work alongside employees to get realistic insight into the struggles they deal with daily on the job. When the boss finally discovers the inevitable shortcomings of their organization, they make suitable changes. The finale includes a grand gesture where select worthy employees receive a big surprise gift based on their situation, such as college tuition or an expensive family vacation. Working alongside them, the undercover boss takes the time to get to know the employee, their work and situation. This is recognition, although the terrible disguises worn by the bosses make it a little less credible!

You can show recognition in numerous ways. People want to be seen and valued. They like to know that they are important and making a difference. There are many ways you can recognize employees. You don't have to go undercover with a wig and later pay for them to go to college to make your staff feel special.

Most of us work because we need to support ourselves and others, but the rewards beyond compensation can create a feeling of well-being that often is more valuable than the monetary value of compensation and benefits.

Here are some ideas for recognition that companies have used successfully, and most of them will not break the bank. They may not be appropriate for every workplace, yet they offer ideas on how rewards can let your employees know they are valued and respected.

Share Good News

- If a member of your team plays a sport, acts in a play, runs a race or does something challenging on weekends or during their time off, you can celebrate, support them and even attend their event.
- Offer an hour off or allow staff to leave early to go holiday shopping. There is often a drop in productivity in the hours

preceding a holiday closure. Making it official sends a positive message that you value and respect your team's family time.

- Bring in treats on team birthdays or throw a small party or gathering when someone gets married, has a baby or celebrates another milestone.

- Have a suggestion process and actually pay attention to the ideas that people come up with. Some companies pay money for good ideas. You may be too close or not close enough to know what could make a difference. Great ideas can come when we listen to those who are dealing with the work every day. Make it fun by offering a reward for the most innovative idea, even if you aren't able to implement it. People can get excited when they are included, and it shows great respect, especially when everyone is allowed to participate.

- Write a note and/or leave a small gift on someone's desk, showing you have noticed their work. A "thank you" for good work is a small gesture that will make a big impact.

- Nominate a weekly or monthly person of value.

- As more companies have social media

accounts, allowing a member to be in charge of the social media posts for a week (such as Instagram or Facebook) gives them an investment that costs very little. Choosing someone who already has these skills and is a trusted member of the team is a win-win for all. It is also possible to put safeguards and checks and balances in place to safeguard your organization's reputation.

- Bring your dog to work. OK, this may not be possible or appropriate, although you could have a photo board with pictures of people's pets.
- Bring the family to work. Open House days are a great way to show family members the organization and its culture.
- Have dress-up or dress-down days.
- Offer vouchers for local coffee shops, restaurants or spas. Even relatively low-denomination gift certificates can make staff feel valued.
- VIP for a day. Whether it's the corner office or the VIP parking lot, or both, show you care by letting the hardest-working member of the team enjoy a taste of the executive life.

Recognition Checklist

Make sure the recognition you provide is:

TIMELY

Don't wait. Give recognition as soon as possible after the good performance takes place. Praise tends to lose its effectiveness with the passing of time.

SPECIFIC

Tell the person exactly what they did that was good. A mere "nice job" really doesn't say all that much. Being specific lets the person know what behaviors to repeat in the future.

SINCERE

Insincere praise is usually worse than none at all. Be honest and open. Tell the person what their performance means to you personally.

INDIVIDUAL

Focus on individuals rather than groups. Fact is, not all team members contribute equally.

PERSONAL

Adjust the style and method of your recognition to the receiver. Some people like public praise; some prefer private discussions. Give "different strokes to different folks." Not sure what they prefer? Ask!

PROPORTIONAL

Match the amount and intensity of recognition to the achievement. Going overboard for small stuff will make people question your motives.

Set a Good Example

As a manager, you might believe that your status means you should automatically get respect. As we established earlier, the aim is that everyone is going to get respect, yet you may well find that those reporting to you are waiting for you to show that you deserve it. So how do we fix this?

One of the best ways you can show respect to your team is by being sure they know what's expected. Starting out with respect is the easiest way to be sure that it is a shared experience.

Get to Know Them

Do you know the people who work for you? Do they have children, pets or other responsibilities that might affect their work or make them occasionally late or distracted? If you know a little about them, you can show empathy, genuine interest and make sure they have what they need to do their best work. We are assuming that you would prefer these people to continue working for you.

Don't Assume

A manager often gave the weekend or evening shifts to those without children, believing it was fair because they didn't have responsibilities and had more free time. This wasn't a written rule or policy. It was a presumption that was unfair and discriminatory, even though legal. If the manager took time to get to know the team and asked what they preferred, she would have learned that many workers with children preferred these shifts or those without kids had other weekend commitments or obligations, such as caring for elderly relatives.

Communication

We all think that we communicate well when, in fact, studies show that people generally rate their communication skills as much higher than others perceive. Though we might be focused on how we are communicating or what message we are trying to get across, we should be interested in how that message is being perceived. What we think we are saying and what is being heard are often two different things.

> " Always treat your employees exactly as you want them to treat your best customers."

— Stephen Covey

Feedback

Waiting to give bad news is never a good idea. Giving employee feedback is usually better sooner rather than later. If your staff member is unaware that they're not meeting your expectations or completing tasks the way you expect, it is impossible for them to course correct. Nudging someone in the right direction is much kinder and more effective than waiting until they are so far down the line that they have passed the point of no return. There is a reason that a pilot continually corrects a plane's course. It's no use waiting until your team member is metaphorically in Paris before you tell them they should be in New York. Explain where they have gone wrong on their work journey. Help them get back on track and encourage them to ask questions so they stay focused. If they are consistently moving in the wrong direction, you may have to look at your communication, systems and procedures.

Language

When it is time to do the difficult work of telling a worker that they are not doing things the way you want them to, respect within your language is equally important. Your language is more than just the words. If you are irritated or annoyed before you go into a meeting, it's likely to show in the way you communicate. Firstly, take a few moments to be calm and focused. Then think about what you will say, avoid using words like "should" or "never." Also, appearing angry or irritated will not create a good outcome. Honestly wanting a positive way forward for all parties and going in with that desire will be much more beneficial. Be sure to let go of any negative feelings or perceptions before going into a meeting or making a call.

Level the Playing Field

Having a chair higher than your team sets the tone for any meeting, showing that you are more important. Creating a feeling of inclusivity is better. Experiment with a different layout that creates a more relaxed atmosphere.

Time

One of the best ways that you can show respect is to give people your time and attention. Everyone is busy. Forcing people to walk and talk in order to get your attention, or taking phone calls and not being present, is not respectful. If you have made an appointment or agreed to meet with a team member, honor their time as you would your own. Listen and be completely focused on them. Hold your calls, close the door, put aside your distractions and hear them fully. Remember that your team members have lives outside of work. Do your best to honor personal appointments and commitments they have to fulfill. As long as this is not being abused, it builds trust when workers feel able to communicate when they need time off.

Praise and Encourage

Set a good example. Show by your actions, not just your words.

Catch People Doing Something Right!

The people who report to you on a daily basis do not know by osmosis that you think they are doing a good job. Recognition for many is as important as a pay raise. When was the last time you sat someone down and told them not only were they doing a good job but exactly what it was about their work that you valued? People love being recognized as well as being rewarded. We all need to feel valued. As the manager, you have a huge part to play. Hiding out in the corner office is not the answer.

Compensate and Promote Where Possible

If it is in your power, do a pay audit or recommend a deserving team member for a raise or bonus. Paying your team what they are worth is literally recognizing their value. One of the best ways to value someone for a job well done is to eventually move them into a new role. A key to growth is to be stretched, and it is easy to hold on to an employee who is doing a good job. You don't want to lose them. The opposite could be the case. By stifling someone's opportunity for growth, you may unintentionally encourage them to look for opportunities elsewhere. Once you have helped a superstar team member move up and on, you can help create the next leader.

You Are a Role Model

It is your responsibility to look out for anyone who reports to you and make sure the rest of the team is respecting them. If you observe rude, disrespectful or discriminatory speech or behavior, turning a blind eye or tolerating it is not acceptable. You are in a unique position to stop the behavior in its tracks by clearly showing that it is unacceptable.

Communicate With Your Team

Truth is, you don't just engage in communication – you rely on it. It's the vehicle you use to:

Inform people of things they need to know to do their jobs;

Instruct employees on the "whats" and "how wells" of the work to be done;

Learn what employees, customers and other departments need;

Clarify expectations, roles, responsibilities and time frames;

Coach direct reports to help them learn, improve and grow;

Motivate your team to higher levels of performance and satisfaction;

Receive and understand input, feedback, questions and concerns;

Correct performance and behavioral problems;

Commend and reinforce employees for doing well.

---

66 Leaders who win the respect of others are the ones who deliver more than they promise, not the ones who promise more than they can deliver."

— MARK A. CLEMENT

Action Items

- Get to know your people
- Communicate
- Reward
- Recognize, praise and encourage
- Give prompt feedback

SHOWING RESPECT FOR CUSTOMERS

Your customers pay the wages, keep you in business and deserve your respect. When airlines announce that they appreciate you flying with them and know that you have a choice, they are acknowledging that there are usually other options available to you. If you do not treat your customers with respect, they may well choose to go with someone else next time.

Yes! It's All About Attitude Again

Whether interacting with customers in person, on the telephone, or even in email or writing, our own mood can affect how we are perceived. In order to behave in a respectful manner with our customers, we must feel respect for them. This can start with getting ourselves in a positive frame of mind. Take a moment to breathe and think about the person you are meeting with or speaking to. This will help encourage respectful communication.

Making sure that customers feel valued and well thought of is not something that can be faked. Even during a telephone call, a customer can sense a feeling of disdain, frustration or impatience. As a true professional, you also need to be a student of human behavior. Customers love to feel special and valued, and you can do this without spending too much extra time and effort. It can even help to make your job more enjoyable and rewarding.

People like people who are like them. The way that we find ways to like people is to create *rapport*. One way we can do this is to discover what we have in common. We can also use our body language to positive effect. You might wonder how you can create rapport with someone if they are on the telephone hundreds or even thousands of miles away. Let's find some easy ways to create that positive feeling.

Two Phone Calls That Ended Very Differently

Customer 1: Ended a call and was left feeling irritated, disrespected and ready to find another place to conduct their business.

Customer 2: Ended a call and felt like they had known the person they were talking to all of their life. They felt completely at ease and had that warm glow that comes with a great experience.

What if you could make sure that all of your customers felt like the second caller? You can, with some easy techniques that just require you to stop, think and sometimes press the reset button.

> Everyone has an invisible sign hanging from their neck saying, 'Make me feel important.' Never forget this message when working with people."
>
> — MARY KAY ASH

Your customer is someone's mom, dad, brother, friend or child. They are giving you the greatest gift—their business. How can you make sure that they not only appreciate your service but like it so much that they keep coming back and also tell their friends?

You have to make them feel **special**, which includes being seen, heard and appreciated. Some calls are straightforward and easy to deal with. Others are more complex. Your customer may have tried everything they could before finally making the call. They may have had difficulty finding the correct number or were kept on hold, cut off, or have a million things going on in the background that you aren't privy to. This really is one of those situations where you have one job— to solve their problem to the best of your ability and let them leave the call believing you did everything that you could.

How to Give Your Customer the Best Outcome.

- Imagine a *person* on the other end of the phone. You may be the only person they have spoken to all day. You have the power to brighten their day.
- Smile and act as if you are dealing with them in person and that they can see you. If you are quietly scowling into the phone or headset, they will sense it.
- Be completely present with no distractions.
- Listen and reflect back so you know that you understand their problem.

- Explain why you have to do things the way you do. For example, if it is a computer issue and your customer is asked, "Have you plugged it in?" the question may appear patronizing. Yet you explain with humor that, yes, many people really do forget to switch it on, therefore you have to ask just in case.

You use a different type of rapport when on the telephone. When you are dealing with a customer in person, you can use aspects of the above rapport-building exercise. This is not about being fake but a way for you to quickly create a comfortable situation where your customers get to know, like and trust you.

You never get a second chance to make a first impression, so the saying goes, so make sure to make a good one. Be welcoming, warm and friendly to everyone in the workplace. This includes a ride in the elevator and each time you pick up the phone. Everyone could be a customer in disguise, and everyone has the potential to be a future one. Another way of looking at it: Treat everyone you meet as if it was your grandmother. Would you say or do things differently?

18 Ways to Make Sure You Create a Respectful Relationship with Your Customers

1. Acknowledge your customers
2. Make eye contact
3. Use their name
4. Smile
5. Surprise them with small freebies, courtesies, gestures
6. Take responsibility for problems they encounter
7. Listen carefully and repeat what they say when they explain a problem or issue
8. Use empathy—consider how you would like to be treated
9. Make them feel special
10. Give them what they need, not what you want to sell them
11. Go above and beyond
12. Follow up and ask if you have solved their problem
13. Ask questions
14. Find something that you have in common
15. Really listen to make sure you understand the problem
16. Observe their body language and see if their words and body are saying the same thing

17. Confirm that you understand
18. Slow down and let them think

Observing Rapport

Go into a restaurant or anywhere people are spending time together and watch how they interact. See if you can figure out which people like each other. It won't take long. You will soon see that those who like and respect each other display it in their body language, their facial expressions and their tone of voice.

Are they looking at or leaning in toward each other?

Where are their hands? Are they in a similar position?

Do they lift their glass to drink at the same time?

Do they look interested in what the other person is saying?

Are they speaking in a similar tone of voice?

What is their face saying? Do they use eye contact? Are they smiling?

How to Lose Customers—Disrespect Them by Using 'Foot-in-Mouth Disease'

Thoughtlessness can lead to lost customers, and familiarity can be dangerous. Be careful to stay on safe subjects and not make presumptions or judgments. Here are some things heard from actual salespeople or customer-service operatives when neutral subjects veered into disrespectful territory.

1) When Discussing the Weather—Usually a Good Rapport-building Opportunity

You had flooding over there? Well, I don't have any sympathy. I mean, at least the water's warm, right? It's freezing here. (This is the **opposite** strategy you would choose to develop rapport.)

2) When Discussing Travel

Oh, I'd never go there. It's full of...(offensive term). I can't think of anything I would want from there. (Who knows. Perhaps that's their favorite place, so now YOU LOSE.)

Respect is Listening to Your Customers

Who would have thought that respecting a customer's desire to have clean and comfortable restrooms could have created a cult-like following for a chain of gas stations? Yet this is what happened when Buc-ee's listened to their customers after asking what they wanted from a gas station. They learned that, above price and convenience, there was a desire for somewhere to "go" when they were on the road. Buc-ee's built a business model around the idea. Now people will travel out of their way to use the luxurious restrooms and often spend money on the Southern chain's branded merchandise, along with their gas. They also show their customers that they respect their workers by prominently displaying pay rates and benefits in their stores. Their well-above-minimum wages help attract new talent. The branding and clever twist on customer service means that families turn what might have been a quick rest stop into a destination, all because of excellent customer service.

What could you do to make sure that your customers feel so respected that they not only keep coming back, but they will go out of their way to come to you instead of going to competitors? One way you can discover this is to put yourself in their shoes the next time you are a customer. Think about the companies that leave you feeling happy and excited to spend your money.

- What was it about the service that made you happy?

Now think about the companies where you felt ticked off, irritated and disrespected.

- What did they do that made you unhappy?
- What could they have done differently?

Now think about how you can use that information to help you respect your customers instead of the opposite. Here are some things that people generally say when they have had a good or bad experience.

When Your Customer Had A GOOD Experience, They Will Tell Others:

They really cared about solving my problem.

He seemed to want to fix the problem.

He acknowledged me as soon as I walked in the door.

She asked if I was happy.

He gave me a discount coupon for next time.

He called me by my name.

She smiled.

They listened to me.

When Your Customer Had A BAD Experience, They Tell Others:

I felt rushed.

My problem wasn't resolved.

They blamed me for the problem.

They were rude.

They wanted to get me out the door.

They said they couldn't help me and didn't offer any solutions.

They didn't seem to care.

Your Customers Expect Consistent Respect

When Mel visited a new dentist, he was friendly and appeared genuinely interested in her and her life, not just her teeth. He chatted about things they had in common, and she imagined she had found a place where she would become a regular patient. They shared a similar sense of humor and the jokes made the appointment an almost pleasurable experience.

A few months later, she saw him at a social event. She

made a jokey comment and expected a conversation to spark, but she was shocked when he rushed past, muttering something about not needing this in his off time. His respectful and friendly behavior only lasted until the patient had left the building. Mel checked her insurance coverage and found another place where she could get her teeth cared for.

As we discovered at the beginning of Mel's story, we often feel more valued when someone really attempts to get to know us. A student of human nature can usually tell when someone is being genuine and wants to know them rather than someone who is just in it for the sale.

When you deliver more than you promise, and not the other way around, your customers will become your fans. Those fans who love what you do and the service they receive will also tell other people.

66 If I made a commitment, I stood by that commitment—and try to make it real. Because when you become leaders, the most important thing you have is your word, your trust. That's where respect comes from."

— MICHELLE OBAMA

Flexibility and Going the Extra Mile

A woman, new in town, arrived for an early morning appointment at the hair salon, desperate for a coffee. She was offered a selection of herbal teas. As much as she liked those beverages, nothing was going to cut it that day like a strong cup of coffee. The receptionist saw that she was visibly disappointed. She inquired about which coffee brands the client normally drank so she could offer recommendations for coffee shops for later. Unbeknownst to the customer, she was collecting the information for another reason.

While the caffeine-deprived customer waited for her appointment, the team member got approval to go to the coffee shop across the street and purchase coffee for the customer. She did not promise this in advance, as she wasn't sure if she could deliver. The arrival of a hot coffee exactly as the customer liked it was a pleasant surprise.

Everyone benefited, she purchased expensive products, left a large tip and told everyone she met of the amazing service. Not every staff member has the autonomy to give this type of service, yet these small touches are what make customers feel respected and valued.

Action Items

- Create rapport
- Have an attitude of great customer service
- Be a problem solver
- Consider what extra thing would make your customers feel special and keep them coming back for more

CONDUCTING RESPECTFUL WORKPLACE MEETINGS

66 When people honor each other, there is a
trust established that leads to synergy,
interdependence and deep respect. Both
parties make decisions and choices based
on what is right, what is best, what is
valued most highly."

— BLAINE LEE PARDOE

Meetings can be a great way for a team to come
together, plan, prepare, communicate and get to
know what is happening within the organization.
They can also be a massive waste of time, so much
so that some companies have all but done away
with them. It is now possible to have live
meetings in different continents and time zones

without attendees ever being in the same room together. These online meetings are often more efficient because they take careful planning to accommodate different teams, and people cannot be kept waiting.

Whether you are attending an online meeting, a conference call or an in-person meeting around a conference room table, there are some guidelines that can help the meeting go smoothly and efficiently.

Respect When Attending a Meeting

Everyone attending a meeting brings their own thoughts, opinions, concerns and unconscious biases with them. For some, it is a battleground where they come planning to win. For others, it's a snooze fest, an opportunity to take an hour or two off work to daydream, doodle or play on their phone. If you are serious about your work and about being respectful, it is your job to behave differently. Here are some guidelines so that you can positively influence the success of the meeting and get something useful from it.

> " Always go into meetings or negotiations with a positive attitude. Tell yourself you're going to make this the best deal for all parties."

— NATALIE MASSENET

Language

Framing your language differently can affect the tone of the meeting and allow creativity to flow. Maybe you did something in a different way before. What did you learn? What worked? What could you do differently this time to make the idea more effective?

Mind your language: Try using *"yes, and"* instead of *"yes, but."* It gives a more positive focus to what you say, for example:

We need to start these meetings on time in the future.

Yes, but last time I was here early and no one else was.

Yes, and it really helps to get us out of here more quickly if we start immediately.

If you are planning on adding a *"but,"* it is unlikely that you are adding anything positive to the conversation.

10 Ways to Be Respectful at Meetings

1. Be on time.

2. Be present and pay attention. This might mean giving yourself a moment to let go of all that is bothering you. Don't bring your baggage to the meeting. If you are daydreaming, there is a chance that you will miss something important.

3. Have what you need with you—notes, preparation and a pen.

4. Be focused on the items being discussed. Don't engage in side conversations, chitchat or irrelevant and distracting conversations.

5. Actively listen. Make sure you understand the point being made before you offer an answer or suggestion. When we are keen to get our point across, we may not be fully paying attention to what is being said.

6. Only contribute if you have something to say.

7. Be open. This is the opposite of rolling one's eyes and exclaiming, "We already tried that and it didn't work."

8. Make notes if you are required to take action from the meeting.

9. Turn off or silence your phone.

10. If conflicts or difficult discussions arise:

- Take a deep breath
- Stay away from personal insults
- Focus on the facts

66 The brain will absorb only what the butt can endure."

— UNKNOWN

10 Things to Consider When Planning Meetings

1. Make sure that the meeting has a purpose and everyone knows what it is.
2. Have an agenda. Make sure attendees can add items and know the protocol for doing so. The reason that meetings are considered to be a waste of time is because they are! If teams are sitting around waiting for something to happen, that is not a good use of time. Wasting time is the height of disrespect.
3. Make sure everyone who is expected to attend has all the information they need. Update with any changes to the schedule or location. Finding out about a meeting

at the last minute, or not at all, is one way to leave a team member feeling disrespected.

4. Clearly lay out the ground rules. Again, sometimes these may be unwritten, which is another good reason to write things down.
5. Will there be refreshments?
6. Can members bring in their own food, or is eating a no-no?
7. Is the meeting location clearly designated so that everyone can arrive on time?
8. Define the duration of the meeting and stick to it.
9. Keep things moving and manage the meeting so it is efficient.
10. Be inclusive. Allow the quiet ones to have their say and limit time allowed to those who talk without saying very much.

> 66 Meetings are the linchpin of everything. If someone says you have an hour to investigate a company, I wouldn't look at the balance sheet. I'd watch their executive team in a meeting for an hour. If they are clear and focused and have the board on the edge of their seats, I'd say this is a good company worth investing in."
>
> — PATRICK LENCIONI

If You Are Presenting or Playing a Key Role in the Meeting

Plan, prepare and have necessary information with you. One thing that people complain about is when attendees don't have what they need in order to successfully participate in the meeting. If you are supposed to read or prepare something before the meeting, make sure that you do. A decision may rely on you having considered certain options, so do your homework ahead of time.

> 66 *Meetings: the positive alternative to work."*
>
> — AUTHOR UNKNOWN

Do We Even Need Meetings?

There is much debate about the need for meetings and, in particular, how long they should be. If time is short, it is possible to have "micro meetings." These are short—maybe 10 minutes or less—where there is one agenda item and a specific decision is made. Another strategy is to have a "stand up" meeting where you minimize distractions and maximize time. Both strategies demonstrate that you respect people's time.

The opposite of this is a more relaxed meeting that is aimed at team building. If a meeting can be scheduled around lunch, or if there is a reward— pastries and coffee for an early morning meeting or afternoon refreshments, fruit platter or cake for later in the day—maybe it can be an opportunity for team members to get to know each other, a social occasion. Just be sure that you get the work done.

A 2019 study, "The State of Meetings Report" by Doodle—the online meeting scheduler, found that the biggest irritations in meetings were:

People who take phone calls (55%);

People who interrupt others (50%);

People who don't listen to others (49%);

People arriving late or leaving early (49%);

People who talk about nothing for a long time (46%).

Lower-level irritations included eating, taking notes on a laptop and not contributing.

Telephone Meetings, Online Meetings and Conference Calls

Although online meetings can save a lot of time and money when people need to meet but are in different locations, they can be extremely frustrating if the technology does not work properly. Make sure that you understand how it works and test all equipment beforehand. Decide if you will need the "mute" button. Triple check if the other parties can hear you, especially if you don't want them to. If you plan to screen share, whether you are using a personal laptop or the work computer, be sure to turn off notifications and pop-ups. If you plan to use an internet browser, be aware that autocorrect can result in embarrassing situations. This can range from awkward—when the auto-complete brings up a shopping channel or a competitor's job posting—to the downright embarrassing if anyone using your computer visited inappropriate websites.

Location

Does the meeting always have to be in the same place? Could you occasionally shift it somewhere more inspiring than the conference room? Some companies have lunches, away days, even a meeting on a boat or a half day at a retreat location, allowing a few hours with no distractions. If you are in a position to offer suggestions, use your imagination. Make meetings fun, as well as useful.

A meeting can be a great time to honor those who have worked hard. You could hand out accolades, share good news, success stories, accomplishments or team achievements. This encourages team spirit and respect between everyone in the group. When possible, depending on your organizational structure, make meetings as inclusive as possible. Though some meetings may be only appropriate for team members who have reached a certain level, there may also be special occasions when you can include most or all of the team. Nothing makes people feel respected more than being included and validated, especially in meetings where decisions about them are being made.

" A meeting is an event where minutes are taken and hours wasted."

— CAPTAIN JAMES T. KIRK, 'STAR TREK'

Action Items

- Be punctual
- Be prepared
- Participate
- Be fully present

RESPECT TECHNIQUES FOR OTHER WORKPLACE AND LIFE SITUATIONS

66 Watch your manner of speech if you wish to develop a peaceful state of mind. Start each day by affirming peaceful, contented and happy attitudes and your days will tend to be pleasant and successful."

— NORMAN VINCENT PEALE

Workplace Respect Begins with Self-Respect

Now you have identified and ensured that you are behaving respectfully at work with a great attitude. What about your behavior at work-related events and outside of work? Being professional and showing respect for others does not begin when you reach your desk or workplace. Consider all the people you encounter on the way to work and outside of work.

The key, of course, is to take your great attitude with you wherever you go and also practice self-respect. When you are at work, you don't always get to make a lot of choices. Employers may tell you what to do, where to sit and when you can eat. In some workplaces, you may not even get to choose when you can go to the bathroom. One thing you can always choose is your attitude.

Professional Appearance

66 You're never fully dressed without a smile," so the song goes, from the movie *Annie.*

Alongside your smile, taking pride in your appearance is a great first step to gaining self-respect. Looking good on the outside has a powerful and positive influence on how we feel. This is not about physical attractiveness or going to work looking like you are on a date. The act of making an effort, of dressing for success, of feeling well-groomed and dressed appropriately for your workplace can change the way you feel.

What You Consume

Taking care of your health is a good step toward self-respect. This can include making sure you are hydrated, eating good-quality food and taking the time necessary to have lunch.

Sleep

Getting adequate rest will allow you to feel good at work. If you are tired and irritable, you are unlikely to command respect or have respect for yourself.

How You Talk About Yourself

Positive self-talk is a major factor in self-respect. If you are constantly telling yourself that you are not good enough, that may become your reality. Practicing powerful, positive statements may seem a little strange at first, yet you become what you think about, and the power of your words is equally important. The act of focusing on what you are good at and speaking positively about yourself will add to your bank of self-respect.

Challenge yourself when you hear negative words or thoughts about yourself. Catch them before you complete the thought and then replace them with kinder alternatives.

Instead of "Oh, you are so dumb. You messed up again," try "Hey, you made a mistake. It's OK. You are only human." Create a kind alter ego. When negative self-talk pops up, you will be ready to hear the more affirming voice.

If you want to get respect outside of work, you will need to give it there, too.

As you begin your day, you will likely encounter many people: a neighbor, drivers, pedestrians and cyclists in traffic, a street cleaner, co-workers in the elevator, servers at the coffee shop, passengers on the train. These are all places where you can practice flexing your respect muscles and your positive attitude.

Respect is also about good manners. These are crucial in our interactions, both in and out of work. There are so many ways that you can practice respect outside of work. Once it becomes a habit, it can make you and everyone you encounter feel good.

10 Respectful Super Powers to Use Anywhere

1. Be kind in all situations and consider how you can make another person's life better.

2. Be courteous. Hold the door open, offer to carry a heavy bag or offer up your seat.
3. Say "please" and "thank you."
4. Show respect, whether you are faced with a king or a cleaner, a server or a celebrity. Everyone you meet deserves respect and dignity. The way you treat people from all walks of life says a lot about you.
5. Cameras are everywhere. Behave as if you are being filmed. Would you be OK with your language and behavior being shown on cable news or YouTube?
6. Respect your surroundings. If you see trash, pick it up. If clothes fall off the hanger in a store, hang them back up.
7. Be honest and have integrity. If you find something that does not belong to you, return it. If you are undercharged or given too much change in a store, alert someone. You will feel so much better when you do the right thing.
8. Be you—all the time. Social media is not an excuse to become your own negative alter ego. Anything you post, share or comment on has the ability to come back to haunt you. No matter how anonymous you may feel from your keyboard, your words have the potential to backfire.

Always pause before posting. If in doubt, don't do it.

9. At social occasions, such as office parties, you are an ambassador for your organization. Be especially cautious when alcohol is flowing at events and social activities. Not everything in Vegas really stays in Vegas, and neither does everything that occurs at the office party.

10. Customer-service workers do not always have the answers or the ability to fix your problem. Always be courteous and thank them for their help. Being rude is not acceptable, no matter how exasperated you feel.

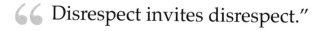 Disrespect invites disrespect."

— MERYL STREEP

Disrespect

The opposite side of the coin and one we must talk about is disrespect in the workplace. The absence of respect is easier to define and notice. When we shine a light and uncover it, we can make sure that respect is restored. Ignoring disrespect helps no one and undermines the good work that is done by companies.

Disrespect can be observed at work as it can be found anywhere people spend time together. In today's instant-gratification world, where it is common for thoughts, feelings and opinions to be shared on social media, if an individual feels disrespected by a team member, a customer or a boss, we will hear about it somewhere. So where did the respect go and how can we get it back?

We often tolerate disrespectful behavior because it comes from individuals we know. Maybe they have been in their position for a long time. Their behavior used to seem OK but now is unacceptable. Yet no one wants to be the one to call it out. "Oh, he's always like that, but he means no harm" or "It's just her way" is cowardly and encourages disrespect and potential lawsuits. This needs to be challenged and handled to foster a diverse and inclusive workplace, especially relating to discriminatory language, comments or behavior.

People who are unhappy can also behave disrespectfully to others. If an employee has experienced disrespect in a past workplace, they may bring that hurt and expectation into a new situation.

A "bad apple" in the workplace can sour the whole team. Narcissistic and unpleasant behavior is dangerous to the well-being of an organization and requires good management.

Unless you have been living under a rock for the past few years, you have probably seen numerous stories about disrespect online. A casual comment, a note written on a receipt, or a face-to-face confrontation can all end up being photographed, recorded and going viral, sometimes reaching the national news before the offender has had time to realize what they said or did.

The old adage, *"Never put it in writing,"* is more pertinent now than ever. It's not uncommon for wait staff to write notes to quickly identify customers. Unfortunately, a hastily scribbled "couple with noisy kids" or "heavyset man with bright shirt" and many far more offensive identifiers never intended for the customers' eyes may cause a huge outcry when it reaches the media, resulting in boycotts, damaged reputations and lost business.

Disrespect can also be found if you look on restaurant, hotel or product review sites. When you take the time to write a glowing review and receive a thank you, it gives you a feel-good factor. That's even more true if you have a bad experience and the organization takes the time to reach out and offer to fix the issue. One of the main reasons that companies have social media accounts is so they can be seen listening to their customers. Many have a team of customer-service representatives whose job is to respond to comments and put out any fires. The person saying they are glad you enjoyed your stay and hope to see you again soon may well be thousands of miles from you and have never set foot in the hotel, yet at least a representative is responding.

Now let's turn to the ones who do answer … A website where your customers can place reviews such as Yelp, TripAdvisor or Facebook can be both a blessing and a curse. Only a small percentage of people who use your services will leave a review. These tend to be split into four categories:

1. Your friends and neighbors who want to support you;
2. People who genuinely love what you offer and want you and the world to know;
3. The disgruntled and those who have had a bad experience;
4. Competitors or those who have a grudge against your business.

Whoever they are, there are two rules that you should follow:

1. Always respond positively.
2. Never contradict.

This can be difficult, especially if you believe that the reviewer is not being truthful. To remain respectful means resisting engaging in confrontations with your customers.

Example

One-Star Restaurant Review

I attended the Happy Fish and was disappointed to find that there was a long wait. When we finally got to our table, the service was slow and the food did not live up to our expectations. The fish was fishy, the soup was watery, and it was raining when we left.

Some people really will complain about things that are out of your control.

Restaurant Owner's Response

(This is a paraphrase of an actual response to a review.)

Our staff remembers the night you came because even though it was a very busy evening, you made yourself known to us and were rude and impatient. You clearly do not understand anything about fine fish or soup, as you probably normally eat in the cheap restaurants in the high street. We have lots of satisfied customers and no one else complained about the food or the rain. This is probably not the right place for you and your family.

What the Owner Could Have Said

We are so sorry to hear that you didn't have a good experience when you came to eat at our restaurant. We would love to give you the opportunity to give us another chance and we will make sure that our service does not disappoint on your next visit. Please send us a private message so that we can help you further.

If you were searching for restaurants in the area, would you be happy to read the first response? Was it respectful? No, of course not. Yet companies can sometimes allow their emotions to get the better of them when responding to complaints.

Customers can usually detect if a review is unfair and will ignore it. They are less likely to ignore a rude representative.

So How Should We Best Respond to People or Online Feedback and Comments?

Here are some ways to make sure you are respectful and keep your cool:

- Take a moment to think about the customer's point of view.
- Never respond when you are angry. Take a deep breath.
- Ask someone to read what you have written so that you get an outside perspective.
- Imagine you are talking to someone you like and respect.
- Ask if there is anything you can do to rectify the situation.
- Use it as a learning experience, making sure everyone responsible for dealing with customers is on the same page.
- Remember that once comments are written and posted, they are there forever. Even if you act hastily and delete your response, someone somewhere may have taken a screenshot. So now more than ever it is vital that everything you say online is done with the utmost respect.

Action Items

Recognize the inherent worth of all human beings.

Eliminate derogatory words or phrases from your vocabulary.

Speak with people—not at them or about them.

Practice empathy. Walk awhile in other's shoes.

Earn the respect of your co-workers through your behavior.

Consider other's feelings before speaking and acting. (This can be a hard one to master.)

Treat everyone with dignity and courtesy.

And, always remember, if you want respect in the workplace.........

You Have to Give it to Get it!

CLOSING THOUGHTS

66 No act of kindness, no matter how small,
is ever wasted."

— AESOP

A respectful workplace encourages
thoughtfulness and affords everyone dignity.
Respect encourages and strengthens teams. A
culture of respect begins with a great attitude. If
you start with that, it's unlikely you will go
wrong. It costs nothing to demonstrate respect
and creates a good outcome for everyone
involved.

The ideas and tips in the previous chapters are
just that—ideas. You will find your own way of
doing it. Your organization has a uniqueness, a

culture and history that will not be found anywhere else. Play to your strengths. Find innovative ways to foster a sense of belonging, a way to draw out the best in each other and to truly value everyone you encounter on a daily basis.

Workplace respect is an ongoing commitment rather than a policy or procedure that can be dusted off when a problem occurs. It is central to a workplace where each part of the team continually challenges themselves to do better. As you work to develop a more respectful organization and strengthen the link between respect, recognition and motivation, you will be part of a place where everyone experiences dignity, care and compassion.

It is important that you now take what you have learned and move it from the page into real life. Turning good information into actions is vital. How many times have you heard someone say, "Well, I was going to do it, but then I didn't?" Think of opportunities where you can show respect and practice having a great attitude in every situation.

Here are some final ways you can practice behaving respectfully in the workplace:

Remember names—Make a point of asking and remembering people's names.

Encourage—Whatever your role in an organization, you can be an encourager.

Share—Information, good news, cookies.

Pause—Before you respond, jump into a conversation or offer an opinion, take a moment.

Empathize—Before making a judgment, think about what it might be like to be in someone else's shoes.

Choose your attitude every single day and adjust it as necessary.

Thank: Be appreciative. A "thank you" can go a long way in showing respect and building relationships.

What Else Will You Do to Be a Part of Creating a Respectful Workplace?

As you give more respect, you will begin to see more of it reflected back to you.

With **Respect in the Workplace, You Have to Give It to Get It.**

Final Action Items

- Attitude is everything. Choose a good one.
- Be thoughtful and kind.
- When in doubt about a behavior—don't.
- Over deliver.
- Remember the human.

Respectfully,

Eric Harvey and Trish Taylor

"Respect yourself and others will respect you."

-Confucius

ABOUT WALK THE TALK

For over 40 years, we have been dedicated to one simple goal...one single mission:

to provide you and your organization with high-quality products and services to ensure individual and organizational success.

Walk The Talk resources are designed to:

• Build critical skills and the confidence to apply them

• Develop an organizational culture that attracts and retains the best of the best

• Deal with workplace *tough stuff* like employee performance problems and litigation avoidance

• Create more trust, confidence and collaboration at all levels

• Help your organization thrive in today's challenging and ever-changing world

Interested in ordering copies of *Respect in the Workplace: You have to Give it to Get it* for members of your organization? Visit Walkthetalk.com

$14.95; quantity discounts available.

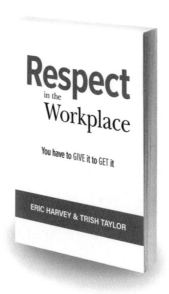

If you have questions or need additional information, please contact us at **info@walkthetalk.com** or call us at **1-800-822-9255.**

ABOUT THE AUTHORS

Eric Harvey is founder of the Walk The Talk company and a leading expert on positive people practices and high-achieving organizations. He has worked with hundreds of organizations worldwide, including multinational corporations, leading healthcare providers, high-tech companies and respected nonprofit organizations.

Eric has authored and co-authored 27 books that have sold millions of copies to include the best sellers *Walk The Talk, Walk Awhile in My Shoes, Ethics4Everyone* and *The Leadership Secrets of Santa Claus.*

Eric devotes his time to writing, consulting and family. He and his wife, Nancy, live in Pensacola Beach, Florida, and are the proud parents of two daughters and six grandchildren. Learn more by visiting walkthetalk.com. Contact Eric at ericharvey@walkthetalk.com.

Trish Taylor was living and working in England, happily settled in her 14-year role as a career counselor and part-time jazz singer. An encounter with a Salsa-dancing American literally swept her off her feet. They married and moved to the United States.

She has worked as an employment coach to individuals with developmental disabilities and later as a mindset coach and trainer. She now writes, speaks and offers trainings and workshops.

She is the author of *Why Am I Scared? Face Your Fears and Learn to Let Them Go* and *I'm Never Drinking Again: Maybe It's Time to Think About Your Drinking?*

Trish lives in Pensacola, Florida, with her husband.

Connect with Trish at www.trishtaylorauthor.com.